THE
ROAD
BACK

THE ROAD BACK

Foundations for a Blessed Life

RICK TOLLEY

The Road Back

Copyright © 2019 by Rick Tolley. All rights reserved.

No part of this publication may be reproduced, stored in a retrieval system or transmitted in any way by any means, electronic, mechanical, photocopy, recording or otherwise without the prior permission of the author except as provided by USA copyright law.

Scripture quotations are taken from the *Holy Bible, New Living Translation,* copyright ©1996. Used by permission of Tyndale House Publishers, Inc., Wheaton, Illinois 60189. All rights reserved.

Scripture taken from the *New King James Version*®. Copyright © 1982 by Thomas Nelson, Inc. Used by permission. All rights reserved.

Scripture taken from the *Amplified Bible,* Copyright © 1954, 1958, 1962, 1964, 1965, 1987 by The Lockman Foundation. Used by permission.

The opinions expressed by the author are not necessarily those of URLink Print and Media.

1603 Capitol Ave., Suite 310 Cheyenne, Wyoming USA 82001
1-888-980-6523 | admin@urlinkpublishing.com

URLink Print and Media is committed to excellence in the publishing industry.

Book design copyright © 2019 by URLink Print and Media. All rights reserved.

Published in the United States of America

Library of Congress Control Number: 2019918594
ISBN 978-1-64753-008-2 (Paperback)
ISBN 978-1-64753-007-5 (Digital)

24.10.19

CONTENTS

Preface 7

A Believer or a Disciple? 9

A Game for the Brave 12

All That Glitters Is Not Gold 16

An Honest Look 18

Can This Be Happening to Us? 21

Chuckin' Stones 23

CHURCH: The Roadblock to Jesus 26

Cockroaches in the Kitchen 29

Let's Make Cookies 32

Get Out the Whip 35

Here's Spit in Your Eye 39

Is This Word for You? 42

Need Bread?	46
Tears of the Father	49
The Call to Arms	53
The Cootie Syndrome	56
The Heart of Caleb	59
The Lonely Place	62
The Real Problem with America	64
The Word: More Than a Book	67
Conclusion	71

PREFACE

I am amazed how many people simply accept what they hear as truth. It is a sad thing that so many have an opinion but can't tell you how they arrived at that conclusion. I guess one could call it laziness.

We grab the first idea that comes across our path that sounds reasonable, and we latch on to it without taking time to think through it ourselves. I have a hard time relating to that line of thinking. I have always been one to question things.

If you are going to be one who questions, you must also be ready to stir up controversy. Over the years, I have enjoyed stirring things up. Am I always right? Obviously not, but if I can get someone to stop and think and evaluate a topic, I have helped them grow in understanding.

Controversy and differences in opinion create a healthy environment to learn and grow. I pray the articles in this book will stimulate you to grow in your understanding of God and His plan. I challenge you to think on it!

A BELIEVER OR A DISCIPLE?

Do you mind if I give you something to chew on? I hear a lot of people refer to themselves as believers in Jesus, but is that who he called you to be? I am sure you have heard it said that even the devil is a believer. So being a believer is not that special.

The term *believe* means to take as true or real, to trust a statement or promise, to suppose or think. Many suppose or think Jesus is real, and they even trust it is true that he is who he says he is. The stark truth is that man*y believer*s will end up in hell. Never once does Jesus call people to become believers.

He does call you to be a disciple; he even makes that the mission of the Church. Matthew 28:19 commands the Church to go and make disciples.

Therefore go and make disciples of all nations, baptizing them in the name of the Father and the Son and the Holy Spirit. Teach these new disciples to obey all the commands I have given you. And be sure of this: I am with you always, even to the end of the age.

Matthew 28:19 (NLT)

I am so amazed that few people who call themselves Christians know or understand what it means to be a disciple.

What is a disciple of Jesus Christ Jesus says in John 8:31, Jesus said to the people who believed in him, "You are truly my disciples if you remain faithful to my teachings.

John 8:31 (NLT)

A true disciple is a person that lives according to the Word of God to the best of their ability. He is not saying to live the way you want and do your best to live a good life. He is not saying just go to church on Sunday and pray when you get in trouble.

The King James Version says we are to "abide in My Word." What does that mean exactly? A true disciple loves the Word of God, is a lifelong student of the Word, is spiritually hungry, and remains teachable.

Be diligent to present yourself approved to God, a worker who does not need to be ashamed, rightly dividing the word of truth.

2 Timothy 2:15 (NKJV)

But don't just listen to God's Word. You must do what it says. Otherwise, you are only fooling yourselves.

James 1:22 (NLT)

According to the Word of God, are you a disciple, or are you merely a believer? A disciple relies on the power of the Holy Spirit to live the life God calls them to. A disciple realizes that they do not have the power or ability to live as Jesus Christ demands without the ministry of the Holy Spirit.

God is issuing a call for you to get back to your mission, and that is the making of disciples. You must understand that to make disciples, you must first be a disciple.

A GAME FOR THE BRAVE

I woke up out of a sound sleep, and I heard two words playing in my head. These two words caused me to tremble and left me with a sense of weakness that I find hard to describe. They are two words that I felt I must put before others for their consideration. I must warn you that if you are brave enough to truly think about these two words, it could change your life completely

What are these two words that are so powerful that they would cause a grown man to shake with fear? The two words I want you to seriously consider are *what if.*

I hear so many mock the Bible, God, and Jesus Christ. In arrogance, they dismiss the Bible as a book of fairy tales. In their pride they live life as though they were in charge of their lives and are free to live as they please. But to all who are so prideful that they think they know best, would you be willing to play the game?

I will share some thoughts with you that will begin with the words *What if?* Are you game?

What if the Bible is Completely True?

Most people who dismiss the Bible have never read it. You may have read parts of it but have never read it cover to cover. Like many things, you may have formed your opinions based on what others have said instead of checking it out for yourself. Have you read the Bible cover to cover? Maybe you have read it, but I challenge you to read it while considering the question above.

What If There Really Is a Heaven and a Hell?

Jesus describes the realities of a place of torment in Luke 16:19–31. I challenge you to read it and ponder the question, "What if the Bible is true?" What would it be like to live in such torment? On the other hand, what would it be like to live in a place of perfect peace?

What If There Really Are Eternal Consequences for Our Sin?

Romans 6:23 says, "The wages of sin is death." This not just physical death; it is an eternal separation from God.

What If Jesus Is The Only Way To God?

Jesus said in John 14:6 (NLT), "I am the way, the truth, and the life. No one can come to the Father except through me." Many say there are many ways to God and not a single way is right. But what if He is the only way and you miss it?

What If There Really Is Life After Your Life Here on Earth?

You may be living your life as though this is it; you live in the here and now, with no thought of what comes after this life. Your life is consumed with the things of this earth. Jesus said in Matthew 16:26, "And what do you benefit if you gain the whole world but lose your soul? Is anything worth more than your soul?"

What If Today Was Your Last Day to Make a Decision, Which Way Will You Believe?

There are no guarantees that we will always have tomorrow to decide. In 2 Corinthians 6:2, it says, "Today is the day of salvation." Today is the time for you to decide.

What If Hebrews 9:27 Is True?

And just as each person is destined to die once and after that comes judgment." Would you be ready to face judgment if today was your last day?

I realize there will be those who will read this and blow it off, but I pray that you have been brave enough to seriously consider *What if*. Jesus came to give you life, and He came to make a way for you and me to know that we will one day be able to stand before God, free. Would you consider one more *what if?*

What If Heaven Is Everything the Bible Says It Is?

Wouldn't it be a shame to miss it? The good news is, you don't have to.

ALL THAT GLITTERS IS NOT GOLD

In the days of the California Gold Rush, people flooded to California with the dream of striking it rich. They called it gold fever. It consumed people; they gave up everything family, life's savings, and their homes. But they discovered something as they scratched and dug into the dirt and rock: all that glitters is not gold.

They discovered something they called fool's gold. It looked like gold, but the truth was, it was worthless. Many people are being fooled by the glitter of things that are really worthless you believe that if you could just hit it rich, you would have it made. You believe that if you could just get the right education, doors of opportunity would swing open wide for you. You may be thinking if I could find the right person to be with, my life would be wonderful. The list can go on and on, but once you obtain them, what do you really have?

You have to face the fact that when it comes down to the end of your life, everything you spent so much time and energy seeking after will not matter. The only thing that will matter is, do you have a relationship with Jesus Christ? Notice I did not say did you go to church, or were you a good person? Do you know that Jesus died for your sins, and have you committed yourself to follow in His footsteps? That is what will matter.

The sad thing is that the church has fallen into Satan's trap and has chased after *fool's gold.* We think that if we have big buildings and a crowd, we are successful. We have pastors who believe that successful ministry is achieved by climbing the corporate ladder of the denomination. The truth is, are you a living demonstration of Jesus to the world around you? Do people think of Jesus when they see your life?

You have one life to live, make certain you are not wasting it by chasing after the glitter. Jesus said that on Judgment Day there will be some who will hear: Well done, my good and faithful servant. While others will hear, depart from Me, you workers of iniquity. You have one life to live; make it count and go for the gold by investing your time and effort in building your relationship with Jesus Christ through spending time in His word, talking with Him through prayer and inviting Him to be part of every area of your life.

I challenge you to invest your life in the things that matter to God. Everything else is *fool's gold.*

AN HONEST LOOK

Your eye is a lamp that provides light for your whole body. When your eye is good, your whole body is filled with light. But when your eye is bad, your whole body is filled with darkness. And if the light you think you have is actually darkness, how deep that darkness is! No one can serve two masters. For you hate one and love the other; you will be devoted to one and despise the other. You cannot serve both God and money.

Matt. 6:22–24 (NLT)

We have heard many sermons on the fact you cannot serve God and money. We are often told that money is the object of this scripture, but I believe this is not the subject Jesus is focusing on. Some, usually those who have little money, use this scripture to condemn those who have money. Those who have money defend their wealth by quoting in part 1 Timothy 6:10, "For the love of money is the root of all kinds of evil." They argue that they don't love money.

What is Jesus really trying to teach you? I believe He wants you to take an honest look at where your focus is. Let's look deeper into this passage. Have you ever tried to focus on two objects at the same time? It is impossible. God created us you to be single-minded with the capacity to focus only on one object at a time.

Jesus said when you focus on the right things, you can expect right results. But if you focus on the wrong things, you can expect wrong results. Where your real focus is determines the outcome of your life. The question you must honestly ask yourself is, where is your focus? The problem most people encounter is they have this terrible problem discerning the truth. You can easily deceive yourself.

He gives this warning: "And if the light you think you have is actually darkness, how deep that darkness is!"(Matthew 6:23). How your heart can deceive you into thinking that what you possess is light, but in fact, Jesus said it is really darkness, a very deep darkness.

He goes on to say that your devotion to one is always at the expense of the other. Money is symbolic of the world and all it has to offer. When you love the world, you do so at the expense of your love for God. When you are devoted to the things of this world, you despise God. You may already find yourself justifying yourself. You cannot afford to justify yourself; you must face the ugly truth, for it is the truth that can set you free.

You may be thinking that somehow, you can get away with doing both. In fact, much of what is preached today says it is a mark of true faith. You often hear that the mark of faith is tied to acquiring of wealth. What a lie of the enemy.

The only way for light to penetrate your life is to walk in the light of God. He must be your entire focus. Wealth or the lack of it has nothing to do with your faith. True faith is focused on God alone. I know this is hard to swallow, but you will have to take it up with Jesus. He is the one who said it, not me.

You have always heard the old saying, "You can't have your cake and eat it too." Friends, Jesus is clearly telling you that you can't have your cake and eat it too. It cannot be Jesus and the world. You must decide where your focus is going to be. You will either follow the Kingdom of God or the kingdom of this world.

Where is your focus? Is your body full of light or darkness? Have you fallen into the deception that you think your darkness is really light? Do you think it is time to take an honest look?

CAN THIS BE HAPPENING TO US?

Except for those who are old enough to remember the Great Depression, most of us have known an America that has never had to really lack for anything. Our idea of hard times would be considered prosperous times by most of the world. I recently read somewhere that if you have a roof over your head, food in your refrigerator, and clothes in your closet, you are among the wealthiest 25 percent in the world.

Many in the world do not know a time when war was not a normal part of life. They live every day in fear for their lives and the lives of their loved ones.

America had grown to expect nothing but peace and prosperity. We believed it was our right to have all we wanted when we wanted it, but all that changed on September 11, 2001. For the first time, we were confronted with our vulnerability. We felt violated. How could this happen to us?

More recently, we have seen our economical superiority in the world drastically decline. We are no longer *the* world power. No longer is the world looking to America to rescue them. We have felt the effects of a global economy, with many jobs moving to other parts of the world. How can this be happening to us? What has happened to the America we once knew?

Though none of us like struggles and tough times, they do not have to be negative. In fact, all we see that is happening could be the best thing that happened to America. Troubles can be a blessing or a curse depending on how you choose to look at it. They can either defeat you, or they can make you stronger. Difficult times force us to look at ourselves, to evaluate what is really important, and to see the need for change.

We have a great opportunity to turn back to God and once again be one nation under God. We have the opportunity to confess our arrogance, thinking that we no longer need God. The only answer for us as individuals and as a nation is God.

Jesus looked over Jerusalem and wept because they had rejected God's love for them. I believe that He weeps for us as a nation, a nation that He has blessed with abundance and influences, only to have us reject Him.

Will this be the downfall of America, or will it be written down in the annals of history as the revival of the greatest nation the world has ever known?

CHUCKIN' STONES

In John chapter 8, some religious leaders brought a woman to Jesus who had been caught in the act of adultery. The punishment for such an act was to be stoned to death. These self-righteous leaders came to see what Jesus had to say. They hoped they could trick Him into something they could use against Him.

Jesus's reaction to the situation seems strange. He bends down and begins to write in the dirt. Many speculate what he wrote; I believe the answer is found in Jeremiah 17:13.

O Lord, the Hope of Israel, all who forsake You shall be put to shame. They who depart from You and me [Your prophet] shall [disappear like] writing upon the ground, because they have forsaken the Lord, the Fountain of living waters.

Jeremiah 17:13 (Amplified Bible)

These leaders knew the message Jesus was giving them. He was telling them that they had turned away from the Lord and were forsaking Him, the fountain of living water. Then Jesus turned the table and told them that the person without sin in their own life was free to throw the first stone.

He then once again stooped down and wrote in the dirt.

The message got through loud and clear. According to the Bible, they one by one dropped their stones and walked away. When they turned their attention from the sin of the woman and looked into their own hearts, they recognized their own guilt. Many of us are quick to look at the sin of others as a way of avoiding a look into our own heart. It is so much easier to throw the stone at someone else than look at ourselves.

Religion is always ready to cast a stone at someone else's direction, but Jesus will not let us get away with that. Jesus did not condone the woman's sin. He did not say it was okay if that was what she wanted to do. If you read it, He actually called her act for what it was—sin. But Jesus always expects us to deal with our own sin first before we look at the sin of others.

So many want to twist this account into saying that we should not judge, but Jesus did judge the sin of the woman by calling it what it was. As Christians we are to judge sin, not the sinner. Notice Jesus told her to go and sin no more. He did not condemn her. He gave her the opportunity to change. Jesus will not ignore sin, but His mercy will give everyone an opportunity to turn from the sin.

Jesus was not condoning the sin, but He was emphasizing the need for all of us to examine our own hearts first. The fact is none of us are in a position to judge others without first judging ourselves. God is the one who will judge. He is the only one who can because He is without sin in His own heart.

Have you picked up stones to cast at someone else because of their wrongdoing? Have you taken the time to examine your heart first? These religious leaders wanted to hold someone accountable to a religious standard they themselves could not meet. As Jesus writes on the dirt, is he writing your name there?

CHURCH: THE ROADBLOCK TO JESUS

Church is the biggest hindrance to people coming to know Jesus. The primary mission of The Church is to bring people to Jesus. Let me begin by defining the difference between church and The Church.

The Church, according to the New Testament, are those people who believe Jesus is all He claims to be and have committed themselves to faithfully follow and obey Him. Their primary goal is to pattern their lives after Him; when people see their lives lived out, they see Jesus and are drawn to Him.

The Church desires one thing, and that is for people to know the love of God through Christ. They don't attempt to "straighten" people out; they leave the "changing business" to the Lord. The Church does not portray themselves as though they have everything together, but as people who are being changed by the Lord. They love others and forgive others just as the Lord has done for them. The Church meets people where they are and comes with the attitude of Jesus. Jesus said, "Just as the Son of Man did not come to be served, but to serve, and give His life a ransom for many" (Matthew 20:28, NKJV). The Church seeks to go out and make disciples of Jesus (Matthew 28:19-20).

Church, on the other hand, is often identified as a place where people gather for religious meetings with others who believe for the most part like they do. Church's primary goal seems to be to recruit others in order to get them to believe like they do. Church has made getting people to church our mission. Church even competes with other congregations to see which one can draw the biggest crowd, Church is constantly looking for new ways to draw people in. Jesus never said, "If church be lifted up, I will draw all men to church."

Church is often full of the tradition of men and looks very little like the New Testament Church in the book of Acts. Too often, church people, in an effort to make a good impression on perspective members, portray themselves as something they are not. They give the impression that they have it all together. This has produced the opposite results; people turn from and reject church. More often than not, when inviting someone to church, the response is negative:

Church attendance numbers ought to be a message that people are not interested in church, but I have found that when Jesus is presented and lifted up, people respond more favorably. It is high time to get church out of The

Church and return to what Jesus commanded us to be. Church will not change lives, but Jesus certainly can.

> I have come as a light into the world, that whoever believes in Me should not abide in darkness. And if anyone hears My words and does not believe, I do not judge him; for I did not come to judge the world but to save the world. He who rejects Me and does not receive my words, has that which judges him- the words that I have spoken will judge him in the last day. For I have not spoken on My own authority; but the Father who sent Me, gave Me a command, what I should say and what I should speak. And I know that His command is everlasting life. Therefore, whatever I speak, just as the Father has told Me, so I speak.
> John 12:46–50 (New King James Version)

Are you ready to give up church to be The Church? People's eternal destiny hangs in the balance. They are waiting for your answer.

COCKROACHES IN THE KITCHEN

I know what you're thinking. Who wants to think about cockroaches? They are disgusting. Did you know that cockroaches are one of the hardest pests to get rid of? They can survive almost anything. They like to live in damp dark places. They emit an odor that is terrible, and they attract other cockroaches.

What does that have to do with anything? I was reading 2 Corinthians 12:20–21:

> For I am afraid that when I come, I won't like what I find, and you won't like my response. I am afraid that I will find quarreling, jealousy, anger, selfishness, slander, gossip, arrogance, and disorderly behavior. Yes, I am afraid that when I come again, God will humble me in your presence. And I will be grieved because many of you have not given up your old sins. You have not repented of your impurity, sexual immorality and eagerness for lustful pleasure
>
> 2 Corinthians 12:20–21 (NLT)

You may continue to struggle with sin in your life, and think that if you ignore it, maybe God will forget about it, or perhaps it will magically disappear. Unfortunately, it won't happen. Like cockroaches, sin will not just go away.

Sin that is not dealt with is much like cockroaches. They like to live in the dark, and every time they are exposed to light, they run and hide. I believe this is why so few people who claim to be Christians spend so little time in the Bible or like good, sound biblical preaching. It turns the light on their sin. I know you may use the excuse you just don't like to read, but it really is just that—an excuse. You who claim that have no trouble reading newspapers or other materials that is to your liking. The Bible says those who truly have a heart for God run to the light, not away from it.

Sin that is allowed to continue to have a place in your life produces a stench in the nostrils of God. God has a great sense of smell. No matter how you try to disguise it, God knows it is there. You think if you offer incense, like attending church as often as you can, pray once in a while, and put a dollar in the offering plate (many put in a dollar because it's too embarrassing to make change out of the plate) that will cover up the unconfessed sin in your life. The only thing that will remove the stench is true repentance.

Sin will multiply; one sin leads to another. Unconfessed sin is like a cancer; it will reproduce at such a rate that will ultimately destroy ("For the wages of sin is death" [Romans 6:23]). It is like lying; if you tell one lie, then you will find yourself having to tell another to cover up the first one. Before you know it, sin has taken over your life.

The Apostle Paul was telling the church at Corinth that they had all this sin, and they refused to deal with it, but he reminded them that one way or the other, they would have to. There will come a time when you will have to face the sin in your life. You will have to stand before God and give an account. I don't know about you, but I believe it will be much easier to stand before Him with a clean record.

When you turn the light on and you see a cockroach run across the floor, you can choose to ignore it as just another bug, or you can keep the light off and pretend they are not there, but believe me, there will come a time you will no longer be able to ignore it.

Don't let cockroaches take over your kitchen, and don't let sin have any place in your life. In 1 John 1:9, it says, "But if we confess our sins to Him, He is faithful and just to forgive us our sins and to cleanse us from all wickedness." I guarantee He is much better than the Orkin man.

LET'S MAKE COOKIES

One of the fondest memories I have as a kid was making cookies. Grandma and my mom both had a set of cookie cutters; I remember there were the stars, bells, and various other shapes. It was always a thrill to make my favorite shape and then get to eat them. My shape always seemed to taste better than anyone else's shape. It was the same dough, but the shape I chose was the best.

When I think of *Churchianity* (our idea of what it means to be a Christian), I think of my mom's cookie-cutter set. We all have our favorite shape that is the best. We have Baptist shapes, Methodist shapes, Pentecostal shapes, and my favorite, the Independent shapes. We think our shape is the best, and anyone who is not shaped like us is just not as good. We like our shape so much that we want everyone to be the same shape as us.

We like our shape so much we will try to convince and convert everyone into our shape. We have not learned that it is not the shape that determines a good cookie; it is the dough. If the dough is right, it really does not matter what the shape is.

Jesus left us the recipe before He left this earth and returned to heaven. In Matthew 28:19–20 (NLT), it says, "Therefore go and make disciples of all the nations, baptizing them in the name of the Father and the Son and the Holy Spirit. Teach these new disciples to obey all the commands I have given you."

First, what is a disciple? A disciple is to be a replica of the original. What Jesus was telling us was to go out and make replicas of Him. He never once said to go make Baptist, Presbyterian, Holiness, or Assembly of God disciples. I think we have lost sight of what we really should be doing. The bottom line is, God is not interested in your shape; what He is interested in is, are you using the right dough?

I believe it is high time we go back to the original recipe. We are to be teaching people how to be like Jesus, not us. My little girl likes to make shapes out of Play-Doh; the shapes look like those made with a cookie cutter, but they really are not fit to eat. Jesus the Master Judge is not going to pay attention to the shape; He is going to pay attention to the taste. He knows if the recipe is right.

What were Jesus's commands that He told us to teach? He only gave two. Love God with everything you have, and to love your neighbor as yourself. He told us to be imitators of Himself. He said everything else hangs on those two. All this other stuff we throw into the recipe is of our own making. Have you noticed when you deviate from the recipe more times than not, it doesn't taste the way it should? You say, "But sometimes you think it tastes better." That may be so, but then it becomes something you have created, and it only resembles the original. I believe God has had enough of our experimenting with His recipe.

I once had a lady in a church in Oklahoma who, for three years, I tried to get her to confess she was a Christian. She would remind me that she was Church of God, her grandma was and her mama was, and that was good enough for her. I am not so sure that impressed God.

How much emphasis are you putting on the recipe? Or are you focusing on the shape? Jesus condemned the religious leaders of His time for trying to make disciples just like themselves. He warned them all they were doing was putting people under the same bondage they were in. I hate to burst your bubble, but none of our little groups have it all right.

How about all of us put away our little cookie cutters and go back to the recipe Jesus left us? As far as the shapes, let's leave that to God. He can make them any way He likes. After all, variety is good.

GET OUT THE WHIP

What is your view of Jesus? You may think of Jesus as this white guy with long hair, long robe, a quiet, soft voice, and this faraway look on His face. You think of love, peace, and gentleness (at least that part is right). But there is another side of Jesus you will not hear about much because it does not sell very well.

In Luke 19, Jesus is coming into Jerusalem to die; He was coming to fulfill His mission. He fully realized that the cross awaited Him. But he did not come into town as a condemned, defeated man. He came into town with a parade. We might compare it to a ticker tape parade. He knew victory was His.

Just before He enters, we are told that He stands on a hill overlooking the city and weeps over the city. He realizes that the very people He came to save would reject the greatest act of love ever offered. He wept because they were headed for a time of great struggle and defeat; they would reject their only hope.

Where was the first place he went when He got into town? He went to church (Jewish Temple), but it was not for a quiet little prayer meeting. When He got to the temple, He pulled out a whip. Why would He need a whip in church? This no place to bring a whip; it is so unspiritual. What took place next was a real shock to everyone. Jesus went on a rampage. He started kicking tables over and chasing people away (obviously, He never read a book on how to grow a church). Why would He do such a thing? It was so disruptive.

Jesus declared to all present, "The Scriptures declare, My Temple will be a house of prayer,' but you have made it a den of thieves" (verse 46). He let them know they had gotten way off track. They had missed the point of being there. Needless to say, He was not very popular with the religious folks that day.

We are living in a time when someone needs to get the whip out in church. We have missed completely the role and function of what the Church is supposed to be. We have worked so hard to make the church accommodating to everyone; after all, we want everyone to feel comfortable. We have sought to create an atmosphere that is not offensive to anyone. We have compromised what we are supposed to be and do in order to bring in a crowd; after all, success is determined by how big of crowd we have.

One person said, "So goes the church, so goes the world." When you look at our nation, you can see the truth of that statement before your very eyes. It is obvious that the strategy of compromise does not work. Our churches continue to decrease in size, but more importantly in influence. We no longer influence the direction of our nation. The standards of God and the Bible, which this country was founded upon, are no longer considered important; in fact, they are ridiculed.

When are we going to open our eyes, but more importantly our hearts, and do a major housecleaning? We need to stop worrying about fitting in and start standing out. We need to be a place where the truth is spoken, even if it hurts and is not politically correct. We need to be a place where the power of God is demonstrated with signs and wonders. We need to be the one place that will not compromise what is right. We need to get back to the Bible and reject all these ways of men and dead religion.

It is interesting that the church we see in the book of Acts never had a church growth strategy other than following the example and commands of Jesus. They stood out and had no problem drawing people. Wasn't it Jesus who said, "If I be lifted up, I will draw all men to me"? He did not say, "Lift up your congregation or your denomination, and I will draw all men to you."

I wonder who has the courage to get out the whip. I wonder who is willing to lay it all on the line. Please don't wait around for it go through a committee or wait until you can get a consensus. Jesus did not take a vote to see if everyone agreed. Will you be one who is willing to stand out from the crowd? Will you be one who is willing to get the whip out? What do you have to lose? Better yet, what do you have to gain?

HERE'S SPIT IN YOUR EYE

Our eyesight is something we take for granted. My daughter Elizabeth has retinal degeneration, and the possibility of her going blind exists. Think about how your life would be different if you could not see. Think about never being able to see a sunrise or the beauty of a blue sky.

In Mark 8:22-26, people brought a blind man to Jesus to be healed. Can you imagine the hope that must have been in his heart? The possibility to see things that he had only heard others describe would now be his to behold.

Many today are blind, though they can see with their physical eyes; they are spiritually blind. They cannot see the truth of God's plan for their life; they can't see the depth of God's love for them. No matter what you put before them, they just can't see it. Jesus came to restore those who are blind that they may see the wonders of God and experience the joy He has for them.

Jesus did something interesting. Notice the first thing He did was take the blind man by the hand. God never intends for anyone to walk alone. He is always ready to take us by the hand. What comfort in knowing that God is willing to walk with you, and He is willing to lead you in the right direction.

But we must also look at the fact that Jesus did not drag the man; there must be willingness on our part.

The second thing Jesus did was to remove him from the village. He led him into a remote place, away from the influences that kept him in blindness. We all have those kinds of people who may mean well but are constantly reminding us things cannot or never will change. Their idea of encouragement is to get us to accept the fact that change will not come.

The next thing Jesus did sounds totally bizarre. Jesus spit in the man's eye. Our response is, "How disgusting," but why would Jesus do such a thing? Sometimes we all need to be shaken up. We need something that will shake us out of our limited thinking. God wants to get our attention. He is willing to go to great lengths in order for us to see clearly.

The result was that the man could only see men as trees walking. Some would be quick to say that it was better than nothing. It was better than before. Many are walking around with partial sight. Can you imagine seeing people walking around looking like trees? Now that would mess with your mind. I know people who live their lives seeing only a glimpse of what God wants to show them.

It may be okay for some people, but Jesus came to restore things completely.

Jesus touched the man for the second time, and it was then that he could see clearly. Our getting to the point of clearly seeing all God has for us and desires for us is a process. There were some blind people Jesus healed who received their sight immediately, but this man required another touch.

With his sight restored, Jesus instructed him not to go back into the village, which had held him back. We have to guard ourselves from those who would love nothing more than to bring us back into the bondage we just came out of.

Are you having a difficult time seeing God's plan for your life? Are you frustrated that what you see does not make any sense? Maybe this message is for you. Perhaps God put this before you in order to let you know it is possible to see clearly. Are you willing to let Jesus take you by the hand and lead you? Are you willing to let Him do what He knows best, no matter how strange it may seem to you?

Can you imagine the joy this man felt? For the first time in his life, he was able to see the wonders of life. The same joy awaits you who will allow Jesus to spit in your eye.

IS THIS WORD FOR YOU?

Do you ever find yourself amazed and at the same time confused by the human race? I never cease to be amazed at people and how they think. People really don't make sense most of the time. They say one thing and do another. They don't say what they mean.

Can I talk to you, those who claim to be Christians? Of all people, you should be setting an example. If anyone should have clear direction as to where one is going, it should be you who claim to know Christ as Savior.

According to Scriptures, the Holy Spirit has been given to you to guide you into all truth (John 14:16-17). So why are you wandering around like you don't know which way to go? I believe the answer lies in receiving the Word of God. The Lord speaks in many ways, but I believe His primary means of communication is through the Bible.

The question becomes, "If the Bible is God's primary way of speaking to His children, why do we spend so little time in the Bible?" I know, people tell me all the time they are just too busy. It is amazing how the hours spent watching TV and playing video games continues to climb. I would not expect those who make no claims to being Christian to spend time reading the Bible, but how can you claim to be Christian and a follower of Christ and rarely read the Bible?

In 2 Kings 22:13, King Josiah, upon discovering the Book of the Law, said,

> For great is the wrath of the Lord that is aroused against us, because our fathers have not obeyed the words of this book to do according to all that is written concerning us.
>
> 2 Kings 22:13 (NKJV)

Years ago I had a church leader (I use the term loosely) who questioned something I had done or said as not being right. When I challenged him to check it out for himself in the Bible, he confessed that he did not read the Bible. Many who claim to be Christians cannot even answer basic questions when pertaining to simple Bible facts.

Many churches no longer have Bible studies because people do not attend them. We have replaced in-depth Bible study with little how-to discussion groups. When are we going to open our eyes? We wonder why our young people are leaving the Christian faith, but what have the adults taught them? We have taught them that there are more important things to be concerned about.

Many pastors have replaced preaching the Bible with warm fuzzy devotionals that can be delivered in a comfortable time slot. After all, people can't sit and listen to even an hour of Bible teaching, but can go home and sit through a whole day and evening sitting before the TV.

I have to admit that I actually feel ill as I am writing this. I wonder what God feels about those who claim to be His children and say they love Him, but will hardly give Him the time of day?

Jesus said to the Church at Laodicea in Revelation 3:15-16,

> I know all the things you do, that you are neither hot nor cold. I wish that you were one or the other! But since you are like lukewarm water, neither hot nor cold, I will spit you out of My mouth!
>
> Revelation 3:15–16 (NLT)

I guess it makes God ill as well.

The time has come for you to stop playing games. Jesus said in Revelation 3:19,

> I correct and discipline everyone I love. So be diligent and turn from your indifference. Look I stand at the door

and knock. If you hear my voice and open the door, I will come in, and we will share a meal together as friends.

Revelation 3:19–20 (NLT)

He goes on in verse 22, "Anyone with ears to hear must listen to the Spirit and understand what He is saying to the churches.

Is this word for you?

NEED BREAD?

In John chapter 6, we see Jesus perform a tremendous I miracle that fed over five thousand people with five loaves of bread and two fish. Everyone in the crowd ate until they were full, and Jesus had leftovers. He instructed the disciples to gather them up, and it was found that they had twelve baskets full.

The people were so impressed with the miracle; we find they have traveled a great distance to get to the other side of the lake to meet Jesus. They wanted to be with Him, but in verses 26-27, Jesus revealed their true motive for following after Him.

I tell you the truth, you want to be with Me because I fed you, not because you understood the miraculous signs. But don't be concerned about perishable things like food. Spend your energy seeking the eternal life that the Son of Man can give you. For God the Father has given Me the seal of His approval.

John 6:26-27 (NLT)

In verse 28, they wanted to be able to perform the miracles like Jesus. Jesus told them the only thing God requires is to believe in Him. In verse 34, they asked Him to give them the bread from God every day. They totally missed the purpose of the miraculous sign. The bread Jesus offered to them was Himself, but all they could think of was bread for the stomach.

You may seek Jesus for what He can do for you; you want Him to give to you in order make your life easier. But Jesus has a far greater purpose; His purpose is to provide you with eternal life. He is calling you to seek Him, not what he can do for you.

What a sad thing if you miss out on the true miracle Jesus came to reveal and continue to seek only temporary relief for the here and now.

In verse 40 (NLT), Jesus tells us the will of God: "For it is My Fathers will that all who sees His Son and believes in Him should have eternal life. I will raise them up at the last day."

God wants to reveal eternal life through His Son and raise you who believe to be with Him. Does God still do miracles today? Yes, He does. Will He do a miracle in your life? Yes, He will. But you need to realize God does not perform miracles in our lives to impress us with what He can do. He wants to reveal His plan for you, and that is to live with Him for all of eternity.

Jesus told those who sought Him for the sake of a miracle only, "But you haven't believed in Me, even though you have seen Me" (verse 36, NLT). You may experience a miracle that will meet a particular need in your life, but if you miss the true purpose of why Jesus came, you have missed it all.

Jesus said in Matthew 6:33 (NLT), "Seek the Kingdom of God above all else, and live righteously, and he will give you everything you need." God will do the miraculous; He will provide for your every need, but you must seek Him, not the miracle. Are you seeking a miracle, or are you seeking the Miracle Worker? When we find the Miracle Worker, we will find the miracles.

You can deceive yourself into thinking that your motives are pure, but God knows your heart. When you truly seek Him with a pure heart that desires His will for your life, He will not disappoint you. It is not a "what" that you need, it is a "who"; His name is Jesus. In Him you will never hunger or thirst again (verse 35).

TEARS OF THE FATHER

There are many who will relate to what I am about to share, if you can't, then for you I praise the Lord. Many unfortunately know the pain as a parent of having your children turn away from you. They have rejected you as a parent; they no longer even acknowledge that you exist. They blame you for everything wrong in their life, and you yourself carry the guilt of past failures. In the case of some of you, you recognize that you truly have hurt our children in the past. You may have even accepted in your heart that you deserve what you have gotten.

Despite the situation today, whether your separation from your children is of your actions or theirs, your heart is no less broken. You think of them constantly and pray that somehow there will be a day of reconciliation. You pray that one day you will know the joy of a tearful embrace that will bring healing to your family. The things of the past will be put behind you, and you will have the opportunity to show the love you have in your heart for them.

When I look at America and the world today, I think of the words of a God who loves His children and desires nothing but good things for them.

I thought to Myself, "I would love to treat you as My own children!" I wanted nothing more than to give you this beautiful land- the finest possession in the world. I looked forward to your calling Me Father, and I wanted you never to turn from Me.

Jeremiah 3:19 (NLT)

Can you sense the deep sadness in the words of God? Can you get a picture of God's heart?

Perhaps John 3:16–17 will make it clearer for you:

For God loved the world so much that he gave His one and only Son, so that everyone who believes in Him will not perish but have eternal life. God sent His Son into the world not to judge the world, but to save the world through Him.

John 3:16-17 (NLT)

God is calling out to those whom He loves to come back to Him; He desires it so much, he was willing to give His Son in order to restore the relationship He longs for. God wants nothing more than to know the joy of a child of His who comes home to Him. Are you one of those wayward children that God is looking for? In Luke 15, we get a picture of Gods deep desire for your return. Jesus tells three stories to reveal God's desire.

In the first, Jesus describes the shepherd who has one hundred sheep, but one is lost; it runs away. Jesus says he will leave the ninety-nine and search for the one until he finds it.

The second story tells of a woman who has ten coins but loses one. Jesus says she will search until she finds it.

The third story is of a father who had two sons; one of the sons wanted to go off and do his own thing. He asked the father for the money he was to inherit, and off he went. The younger son went out and lived it up until he had lost everything. He even found himself standing in the middle of a pigpen feeding hogs to try and make ends meet. He began to think of what it was like back home, he began to think of all that he had given up, and most of all, he began to think of his father and how much his father loved him. He longed for home. The Bible says he came to his senses and decided no matter what he had to do, home was still the best place to be.

Jesus gives us a beautiful picture of the fathers love for his son. Look at verse 20:

> So he returned home to his father. And while he was still a long way off, his father saw him coming. Filled with

love and compassion, he ran to his son, embraced him and kissed him.

Luke 15:20 (NLT)

The father never stopped looking down the road with the hopes of one day seeing his son return.

God is doing that with those who have left Him and went off to live their own life. He is sitting on the porch, so to speak, and He is looking down the road for you. He longs to see you coming, and He will receive you like the son in the story. He will come running to you and embrace you and kiss you.

Do you ever feel like the son? You feel like you are standing in the middle of a dirty pigpen surrounded by stinking pigs. Your heart longs for home and the embrace of a loving Father. Isn't it time to throw down the pig bucket you are hanging on to and return home? Your Father is waiting for you.

THE CALL TO ARMS

Have you ever heard people say, "This world is falling apart, and somebody needs to do something"? The greatest tragedy is not that things are falling apart because the world has always been in a mess, but the real tragedy is the Church has not stepped up to bat.

The Bible says we have been given power to tread on snakes and scorpions and over every work of the devil; Jesus even goes on to say in the same verse, "Nothing shall by any means hurt you" (Luke 10:19), and yet we sit by and watch Satan have his way.

God gave the prophet Ezekiel a vision of a valley full of dry bones (Ezekiel 37). They were lying everywhere, but something began to happen. God began to move, and when He did, the bones began to rattle and then come together. God asked Ezekiel, "Can these bones live?" (verse 3). But we need to see why God moved. Look at verse 4; God told Ezekiel to prophesy over the bones. God told him to command the bones to hear the Word of the Lord.

We have been told to keep silent; we have been told to keep our *religion* to ourselves. We have been told people don't want to hear the Bible; we have been told not to push the Bible. So we have listened to mere men and rejected the command of the Lord. We have allowed men to silence the very thing that will bring life to the dead, dry bones.

Christian, it is time to once again declare with boldness the Word of the Lord. The Word needs to be proclaimed throughout our land, from the pulpits and from every street corner. Our only hope is for the Church to rise up and arm ourselves with the Word of God, to declare with boldness and the authority Jesus gave us.

When the prophet prophesied, the Spirit of the Lord moved and began to breathe life back into the dry bones. Is the Word of God any less powerful today? Will God not honor His Word today as He always has? I believe He will.

We have taken God's Word out of our schools, and we see an entire generation dying before our eyes. We have taken God out of our government, and we have seen a flood of greedy selfishness rise to the forefront. What will it take for the Church to open our eyes?

When Ezekiel did what he was commanded to do, God did what He promised He would do, and what was the result? Verse 10 says there arose a mighty army; in fact, the Bible says an "exceedingly great army" rose up.

We need more than ever an exceedingly great army to rise up. We need the Church that actually believes Romans 1:16 (NLT): "For I am not ashamed of the gospel of Christ, for it is the power of salvation for everyone who believes."

> If My people who are called by My name will humble themselves, and pray and seek My face, and turn from their wicked ways, then I will hear from Heaven, and will forgive their sin and heal their land. Now My eyes will be open and My ears attentive to prayer made in this place.
> 2 Chronicles 7:14-15 (NKJV)

God does not change; what He said then is just as much for today as it was to the children of Israel thousands of years ago.

Come on, fellow believers. The time is now to take up the Sword of the Spirit and march out with power to declare the Word of the Living God. Will you answer the call?

THE COOTIE SYNDROME

When I was a kid in school, it was often said that no one wanted anything to do with someone if that kid had *cootie*s. As kids, we did not realize how cruel that was. We would scold our kids if we heard them say such a thing. But I believe that the Church has been infected with the "cootie syndrome."

So many Christians are infected with this dreaded disease. What is it? I hear Christians talk about certain groups of people as though they are untouchables. Sad to say many have a set of standards that they expect those who attend their church fellowship to have. If they don't measure up, then they are not wanted.

How does your church fellowship measure up? Has this horrible thing invaded your church? What would happen if someone showed up on Sunday morning in dirty, smelly clothes? What if they were wearing a tank top and flip-flops or pants with holes? Heaven forbid if they came into church smelling like alcohol or under the influence of something. How would they be treated? Would they be welcomed with open arms? Let me ask you another question: does your church go out of your way to reach out to these people?

How would Jesus treat them? I know I am asking a lot of questions, but it is time we ask ourselves, why are we really here? Jesus came to minister to the hurting, the rejects of society, those whom the religious people wanted nothing to do with.

I challenge you to read through the four gospel accounts (Matthew, Mark, Luke, and John) and take note of the people Jesus had the most contact with. Did He hang out with the social elites, or was it the down-and-outers?

When this syndrome invades your fellowship, it may show up as having a negative view of others who claim to be believers in Jesus Christ but come from other denominations. We have groups within the Body of Christ who will not fellowship with other believers.

Years ago, I had begun talking with a man at a restaurant, and it became almost a weekly thing. We would talk about Jesus and would have some great uplifting conversations until one day I mentioned I believed and practiced a certain spiritual gift. The man immediately responded as though I had cooties. He let me know in no uncertain terms because of my belief in this particular gift we would not be having any further fellowship.

Jesus hung out with lepers, prostitutes, thieves, adulterers, and anyone else the modern church in America would consider undesirables. The Apostle Paul hung out in the marketplace and spent hours talking with those who practiced other religions. The Lord told Peter to go to the house of a Gentile.

> For God so greatly loved and dearly prized the world that He [even] gave up His only begotten (unique) Son, so that whoever believes in (trusts in, clings to, relies on) on Him shall not perish (come to destruction, be lost) but have eternal (everlasting) life. For God did not send the Son into the world in order to judge (to reject, to condemn, to pass sentence on) the world, but that the world might find salvation and be made safe and sound through Him.
>
> John 3:16-1 (Amplified Bible)

What would happen if churches and individual believers removed the cootie syndrome? How do you think people would receive your message if they knew that no matter what, they would be loved as Jesus loves? I would venture to say you would not have empty pews.

THE HEART OF CALEB

Most people have as their goal in life to come to a point that will allow them to rest and enjoy the fruits of their labor. We call it retirement. It is the motivating force throughout their working years.

I am one who does not look forward to retiring; retirement is usually the last step before death. This retirement mentality has taken over the Church. Far too many in the Church just want to sit back and enjoy God's blessings. They have bought into the lie that somehow their work is done. They no longer do the things God has commanded them to do. They no longer have a passion to see others come to know Christ. They no longer desire to make disciples. After all, it is time for someone else to step up to the plate.

In Joshua 14:6-15, I am inspired by a man named Caleb. Caleb was eighty-five years old at the time and far beyond retirement age. He stands out because he had a different heart than most people. He comes to Joshua to remind him of how forty years earlier, when on a scouting mission, they saw a land that flowed with milk and honey.

Caleb witnessed something that stirred his heart. It was one of those things that he could not and would not let go of.

He came back to report to the others and Moses that though there were giants in the land; it was worth the fight to conquer this bountiful land. He was willing to take on the giants in order to experience the promise of God. A dream was planted in his heart that someday he was going to have that land.

I believe God is raising up those who have the heart of Caleb in the Church today. Perhaps you possess the heart of Caleb. You have a clear picture of what God promises in His Word, and you refuse to be intimidated by the giant obstacles that stand in the way. You cannot shake the intense desire to experience all God has promised.

I love what he says to Joshua in verses 9–12:

So that day Moses solemnly promised me, 'The land of Canaan, on which you were just walking will be your grant of land and that of your descendants forever, because you wholeheartedly followed the Lord my God' Now as you can see, the Lord has kept me alive and well as He promised these forty five years since Moses made this promise-even while Israel wandered in the wilderness. Today I am eighty-five years old. I am as strong now as I was when Moses sent me on that journey, and I can still travel and fight as well as I could then. So give me the hill country that the Lord promised me. You will remember that as scouts, we found the descendants of Anak living there in great walled towns. But if the Lord is with me, I will drive them out of the land, just as the Lord said.

Joshua 14:9-12 (NLT)

We need some people who have the heart of Caleb those who will not let go of the dream God has placed in their heart. They cannot and will not let go of the promise God made to them. They are determined to see it come to pass. They are relying on the power and faithfulness of God to see it happen. They are not intimidated by the giants who stand in the way. They refuse to lie down and quit.

Are you one of those whom God is raising up and possess the heart of Caleb? Do you refuse to quit until you have laid hold of God's promises? Ask God to give you a clear vision of His promises and give you the heart of Caleb to see all of those promises come to pass.

THE LONELY PLACE

We spend our whole life trying desperately to be accepted by those around us. We want to fit in; no one wants to be an outsider. In our attempt to be individuals, we find ourselves sucked into the trap of being like everyone else. If you have not noticed, even when it seems like we have been accepted, we still battle with the terrible loneliness of an empty heart.

There is a lonely place that can bring you great satisfaction and fulfillment. It cannot be found in the crowds or when you are surrounded by even those you love and admire. It is found in the secret place of the Lord. Psalm 91 calls it the "shelter of the Almighty."

You live such a hectic life, and the pressures you find yourself battling can be overwhelming. You see all around you many who are crushed every day under the pressure. You can see all around you the evidence of what this world and its demands do to people's lives. You may be carrying the scars of such a life, but the good news is that God has created a lonely place for you to go.

Jesus often retreated to the lonely place to be alone with the Father. It was there He found renewed strength and comfort to face the demands of another day. Jesus called it a closet. Do you have a lonely place that you can retreat to and spend time with the Father God?

You may be willing to do anything to avoid being alone, even things you will later regret. But it is in the lonely place you will find exactly what we need. In the midst of all the turmoil, God is calling you to come away with Him. Read the ninety-first psalm and see if that lonely place God is calling you to might not be what your heart needs more than anything.

I have come to find that I cannot cope with life without withdrawing to the secret place of the Almighty on a daily basis. I am so thankful God loves me so much that He has time for me, and He has provided a lonely place for me to go. He has one waiting for you, and if you will quiet your heart and listen, you will hear Him say in the roaring demands of your life, "Come away with me."

He desires to draw you under His wing to experience safety. He wants you to know that in Him, you will sense your fear vanish, and you will experience security only He can provide. He will give you strength beyond anything you can imagine.

Thank you, Lord, for the lonely place.

THE REAL PROBLEM WITH AMERICA

Is our real problem rising gas prices? Is our real problem out-of-control spending? Is it the deliberate push toward socialism? I could go on and on with issues that we face as a nation, but they are merely smoke screens that hide the real issue. Many will laugh and mock what I am about to say, but time will tell.

The real problem is that we have turned our back on God, and He has honored our request to get out of our lives and our nation. We have boldly declared that we don't need Him. Our only choice is to depend on ourselves, and look at what good that is doing.

The sad thing is, the reason the nation has moved from God is because the Church-the Body of Christ-has moved from Him. The Church has sought the approval of the world with great intensity. We have become seeker friendly; we have developed a message that will no longer bring conviction to the hearts of people. Our message of cheap grace, blessings, and prosperity fit right into a nation whose heart is consumed with a self-seeking, self-centered mind-set.

Isaiah 29 gives a clear description of the Church today. Look at verses 10-13:

> For the Lord has poured out on you a spirit of deep sleep. He has closed the eyes of your prophets and visionaries. All the future events in this vision are like a sealed book to them. When you give it to those who can read, they say, "We can't read it because it is sealed." When you give it to those who cannot read, they will say, "We dont know how to read." And so the Lord says, "These people say they are Mine. They honor Me with their lips, but their hearts are far from Me. And their worship of Me is nothing but man-made rules learned by rote.
>
> Isaiah 29:10-13 (NLT)

In Isaiah 30:8-11, we find the message proclaimed by the people pleasing Church of today.

> Now go and write down these words. Write them in a book. They will stand until the end of time as a witness that these people are stubborn rebels who refuse to pay attention to the Lord's instructions. They tell the seers, "Stop seeing visions!" They tell the prophets, "Don't tell us what is right. Tell us nice things. Tell us lies. Forget all this

gloom. Get off your narrow path. Stop telling us about your Holy One of Israel.

Isaiah 30:8–11 (NLT)

Even sadder is the fact that those who stand in the pulpit have conformed to their request. They have watered down the message of the Bible to draw crowds and protect their jobs. The call to preach the Word is not a job; it is a commissioning by Almighty God.

The time has come for those who are called by His name to return to Jesus. Our only hope is humble repentance. Is it hopeless? No! God says He will raise up a remnant who is not ashamed to stand in the last days and proclaim with boldness the message of God. The question is, "Are you one of those who will stand?"

Revelation 12:11 says,

And they defeated him by the blood of the Lamb and by the word of their testimony. And they did not love their life so much that they were afraid to die.

Revelation 12:11 (NLT)

THE WORD: MORE THAN A BOOK

How you and I perceive the Word of God is crucial to our understanding of the Christian life. If we miss the true understanding of this, we can never understand the rest of Scriptures. We must deal with our perception of the Word.

Some believe that the Bible (God's Word) is a book about God and, like any book, is open to human interpretation and reason. Thus they find it difficult to believe it entirely. This is the view of most people, even those who claim to be Christians.

But in John chapter 1, we find the clear teaching of what the Word is. The first thing is that the word is not a what but a who. John chapter 1 lays the foundation for truth. The Word is Jesus. The Word is God.

When we read the words of the Bible, we must see it not as words on a page but as God Himself. Words are merely pictures of the subject. Words are a way of painting a picture for the mind to comprehend. The Bible is God painting a picture for us to see who He really is.

God's greatest desire is for people to see and understand who He is. It is for that reason Jesus came. He came to show us the Father. Jesus said, "If you have seen me, you have seen the Father."

So the Word became human and made His home among us. He was full of unfailing love and faithfulness. And we have seen His glory, the glory of the Father's one and only Son.

John 1:14 (NLT)

We see that there can be no separation from the words written on the page of your Bible and Jesus because both are God.

In John 1:1-4, we get a clear understanding.

In the beginning, the Word already existed. The Word was with God, and the Word was God. He existed in the beginning with God. God created everything through Him, and nothing was created except through Him. The word gave life to everything that was created, and His life brought light to everyone.

John 1:1-4 (NLT)

In verses 10–11, we see that "He came into the very world He created, but the world didn't recognize Him. He came to His own people, and even they rejected Him."

How sad that the very people God created cannot even recognize their Creator when He came to live among them.

Stop and think for a moment, how do you view the Word? If you see it as only a book about God, you will be able to take it or leave it. At best you will read it to know more about God. But the Word exists that you may know Him. In your hands, you hold God. You hold the treasure and the key to know God personally and intimately.

I challenge you to read the words on the pages of the Bible from a different perspective. Ask God to reveal Himself as you read, and you will see Him. You will fall in love with God. You will find a new hunger for Him. Your eyes of understanding will be opened to the wonder of who God is.

My prayer for you is found in Ephesians 1:16–17:

I pray for you constantly, asking God the glorious Father of our Lord Jesus Christ to give you spiritual wisdom and insight so that you might grow in your knowledge of God.

Ephesians 1:16-17 (NLT)

Paul goes on to pray in verse 19:

I also pray that you will understand the incredible greatness of God's power for us who believe Him.
Ephesians 1:19 (NLT)

The Bible—just another book? I think not.

CONCLUSION

As you have taken the time to read through the pages of this book, I pray you have been challenged to stop and think. But more importantly, I pray you have opened your heart to God.

Don't copy the behavior and customs of this world, but let God transform you into a new person by changing the way you think. Then you will learn to know God's will for you, which is good and pleasing and perfect.
Romans 12:2 (NLT)

I pray you have been stirred to an increased hunger to be more like Jesus and experience all He has for you.
Let me close with the prayer Paul prayed for the believers in Ephesus.

Ever since I first heard of your strong faith in the Lord Jesus and your love for God's people everywhere, I have not stopped thanking God for you. I pray for you constantly, asking God, the glorious Father of our Lord

Jesus Christ, to give you spiritual wisdom and insight so that you might grow in your knowledge of God. I pray that your hearts will be flooded with light so that you can understand the confident hope He has given to those He called- His holy people who are His rich and glorious inheritance.

I also pray that you will understand the incredible greatness of God's power, for us who believe Him. This is the same mighty power that raised Christ from the dead and seated Him in the place of honor at God's right hand in the heavenly realms. Now He is far above any ruler or authority or power or leader or anything else, not only in this world but also in the world to come. God has put all things under the authority of Christ and has made Him head over all things for the benefit of the church. And the church is His body; it is made full and complete by Christ, who fills all things everywhere with Himself.

Ephesians 1:15-23 (NLT)

www.ingramcontent.com/pod-product-compliance
Ingram Content Group UK Ltd.
Pitfield, Milton Keynes, MK11 3LW, UK
UKHW022209230426
12048UKWH00016BA/729